Sincerely yours
Carl Starker

S0-CPR-276

WESTERN FLOWER ARRANGEMENT

Photographs by courtesy
of OREGON JOURNAL in
whose Garden Magazine
Section, Carl Starker's
flower arrangements reg-
ularly appear.

WESTERN
FLOWER ARRANGEMENT

By

CARL STARKER

Binfords & Mort, Publishers
Portland, Oregon

COPYRIGHT, 1947, *by* BINFORDS & MORT
* *

Printed in the United States of America

by

Metropolitan Press, Portland, Oregon, U. S. A.

Introduction

THE art of flower arrangement is still in its formative period. Older ideas are being discarded and new practices developed which have done much to clear up the haze of rules and laws that in earlier stages hindered the proper development of this delightful subject.

We have principles that guide just as much in this as in other forms of art. Good design, balance, line, pleasing color, mass and proportion are of utmost importance and must be well considered if one is to arrange flowers effectively.

There are no hard and fast "rules," and good flower arrangement need not be difficult in spite of what some lecturers and judges try to tell us.

This book is written with the hope that the simplicity of its presentation will make it readily usable for the modest home owner and arranger.

Appreciation of beauty is not dependent on money or lack of it. The "seeing eye" will find beauty in unexpected places. If we can stimulate the urge to create beauty with materials at hand, our aim will be accomplished.

We will attempt to show that inexpensive containers and simple garden or roadside material can be as attractive as more expensive flowers if one has the proper feeling for assembling them effectively. A real appreciation of texture and color together with the use of the right combinations of materials will do much to develop an interesting technique.

Much has already been written on the subject. The following books are heartily recommended to the reader.

"Design in Flower Arrangement" by John Taylor Arms.

"Pleasures and Problems of Flower Arrangement" by Emma H. Cyphers.

"Flower Arrangement for Everyone" by Dorothy Biddle and Dorothea Blom.

"Creative Flower Arrangement" by Dorothy Biddle and Dorothea Blom.

"Flower Arrangement in Color" by Rockwell and Grayson.

"Let's Arrange Flowers" by Hazel P. Dunlop.

The subject of color as presented in Rockwell and Grayson's and Mrs. Cyphers' book are especially worthy of careful study.

CHAPTER 1

General Discussion

IF you are to make good arrangements, you must know what flowers to cut and when to cut them. The ideal time is in the early morning while dew is still on the blooms, but evening is also a good time, for the flowers can then be allowed to stand all night in deep water before they are arranged.

Select only buds and freshly opened flowers. Cut with shears or a sharp knife, with a clean slanting cut. If the stems are cut in this manner they will absorb more water, and there will be no danger of the cut ends of the stems resting on the bottom of the pail and failing to take up water.

Blooms should always be hardened off in deep water before they are put in an arrangement. In this way the stems will be filled and they will be able to stand up well, even if a shallow container is used. Many flower stems will take on interesting curves if left in deep water for some hours.

Quite often flowers which were cut in bud will open into more delicate blossoms in the house than if left to mature on the plant. Look for interesting curved stems. They will often set the scheme for the whole arrangement. Do not be afraid to sacrifice length of flower stem to the perfection of your arrangement.

If you are reluctant to sacrifice stem length or the perfection of some certain bloom, use it as a specimen and choose some less perfect flower for your arrangement.

If possible have a cutting garden for growing arrangement material. Many garden flowers are miserable garden specimens.

For your cutting garden be efficient and grow only those types of flowers which will harmonize with your household setting. Study your upholstery, drapes and walls as a guide for color schemes.

Woody-stemmed flowers like chrysanthemums will keep better if the stems are crushed for several inches above the base. Many shrubs will last better if the stems have been pounded or the bark split. Hollow stemmed flowers such as poppies, gerberas and dahlias should have their stems dipped in boiling water for a few minutes before they are put in deep water.

If you are buying flowers, there are several things to remember. Such flowers as asters, lilacs, glads, chrysanthemums and zinnias will last longer than many others.

If you buy flowers which are at the height of their season you will be apt to get fresher blooms than if you buy out of season flowers. If you are a steady customer of a reputable store, you will be less apt to have old, faded flowers foisted off on you.

Fresh roses and other flowers should feel crisp to the touch, like fresh lettuce. This is true of all flowers except stocks. If the color of the flower seems faded, it is a pretty sure sign that they are old.

Do not choose freshly cut flowers that have not been hardened off in water, as they will not hold up well. Don't buy wilted flowers thinking they will freshen up in water. They almost never do.

Study the shape and texture of leaves carefully. They play a very important part in the excellence of your flower grouping. Leaves of strong, definite shape, such as those of the yucca or day lily, or iris will often set the tone of your whole arrangement. Softer, less harsh leaves, such as those of the purple plum, saxifrage, mullein, dusty miller or lambs ears, lend variety and often help in toning down a color scheme and in tying a composition together.

The use of a dramatic leaf or two will often give distinction to an otherwise mediocre grouping. Use restraint.

Fruits can be used only in a fruit arrangement to good effect, or in conjunction with flowers and foliage. A focal point of fruits and foliage in a flower arrangement can be charming and dramatic.

Evergreen blackberries since they can be had in all stages of development at once, ripe, green and in blossom are delightful to use. Quinces, cherries, crabapples, gooseberries, plums, mountain ash, cotoneaster, snowberries and many others give variety.

Vegetables such as gourds, squashes, egg plant, radishes and others are excellent arrangement material. Color and imagination is what you need here.

There are many seed pods of interesting shape, color and texture. Sumac, pepper berries, honesty, sour dock, wild spirea, Siberian irises, anemone pulsatilla, clematis and passion flower, are only a few which could be mentioned for variety. These will find good use in their green state or when partly or fully matured. Their forms and color shadings will do much to pep up a dull grouping.

Webster says that "Design is a plan, an idea intended to be expressed in visible form." *Design* is one of the most important principles of flower arrangement. How often at flower shows or in homes do we see an "arrangement" that is totally lacking in that one point! There is often no sign of planned grouping of material—no idea or plan in the mind of the arranger and so the effect is lost, even though a good container and excellent material is at hand.

Whether we are conscious of it or not, all *good* arrangements must have design. A true flower arrangement must make a composition. It will have design, and not be just a bunch of flowers stuck into a vase. There must be a studied relation between its component parts.

Every flower arrangement should be a picture painted with living material — a pattern of form and color against a proper background. There must be a pleasing sense of line and rhythm. It should constitute a unified whole which expresses the individuality of the arranger. That is why it is so bad to slavishly copy an arrangement which you have seen someone else make, or one pictured in a book.

Before starting an arrangement we should decide what form it is to take. Whether we realize it or not, all designs fall into some geometric shape. There are circles, crescents, fan shapes, many forms of triangles, spirals, Hogarth curves, as well as rectangles and ovals.

Do not get into a rut and always use the same form for your arrangements. There are many other possibilities to try out. Have some fun, experiment a bit, perhaps you will evolve a much more effective style than the one you were wearing threadbare!

No matter what form you use for your grouping you must be careful to have a proper *balance*. This not only means flowering material but container and base as well.

The subject of height in relation to balance used to excite the judges at our flower shows. The old "rule" was a very careful 1½ times the height of the container and many an excellent grouping failed to win a prize if it did not exactly measure up to this rule. We have now grown away from this exact measurement idea. Often 2½ or 3 times the height is needed to properly balance a grouping.

Much depends on color, both in material and vase, and shape as well as weight will influence good proportion. Common sense will determine this usage. Proper distribution of color is essential.

Both sides of the arrangement should appear of equal weight. This does not mean they should be just alike, but they should balance each other. Darker colored flowers appear to be heavier than lighter toned ones. Flowers at a distance from the center of the arrangement appear heavier than those near the center. Use buds and partly opened blooms at the edge of your grouping with the wide open flowers at the center for easier balance.

We may have *symmetrical balance* by having both sides of the arrangement as nearly alike as possible by using approximately the same kind of material or that of the same apparent weight. This gives a formal and often monotonous effect.

A symmetrical balance is achieved by an apparent equality in weight although the two sides of the arrangement are dissimilar. If one side is built high with fairly light weight material, it must be balanced by a smaller amount of heavier material placed low down on the other side.

In every arrangement there should be a *focal point,* or *center of interest,* — a place near the rim of the container from which the design seems to grow. This should be the one dominant note that will hold the interest of the beholder. Here is where the brightest color mass, or largest flower is used. Without a center of interest your arrangement lacks pep and point.

Unity is an essential element in design. Unity in an arrangement means that each part contributes to the whole effect, but is not too prominent in itself. Highly polished or brilliantly colored or figured containers are apt to prove a stumbling block to unity and good effect.

In our high school days when we studied rhetoric we learned that the paragraph must have unity, coherence and emphasis. Just so with a flower arrangement, it should have these same qualities.

Your container and the material contained should make a complete and unified whole. The container must be suited in color and texture and be of a pleasing form to properly set off the flowers and foliage used. The container should not be either too large or too small. Scale and proportion are of the utmost importance. Very often the line of the rim of the container should be broken with a leaf or spray of flowers. This tends to promote unity of feeling by tying the container to the flowers.

A feeling of *rhythm* is often a great help in creating interest in a grouping. The sweep of certain repeated curving stem lines will often set the rhythm or upward movement. The use of straight lines in varied lengths will create an ascending rhythm which gives a feeling of aspiration. We may have color rhythm in a movement of values from light to dark.

Proportion is the relation between the plant material and the container, and between the different kinds of material used. The space where a finished arrangement is to be placed will help decide its height and width and should be well taken into consideration if the best effect is to be obtained. Good line, balance and proportion will be the determining factors in this regard.

Good line is imperative in an arrangement. It should contribute to the interest of the composition. In a mass arrangement it would be defined as a silhouette. There should be interesting voids as well as solids so that the eye of the observer follows around the whole outline of the grouping. Irregularity of outline adds interest. Be careful of your dominant and subordinate lines. The dominant line sets the whole scheme of the arrangement, and determines whether it will be good, bad or mediocre. All other lines must be subordinate to the main one, or re-emphasize its character. The good lines of an arrangement should not be obscured by the use of minute fuzzy flower forms.

Texture is important. It should be pleasing to the eye and blend well. There should not be too wide contrasts in material textures. Textural values of background, container and material should be well considered. You feel textural interest or the lack of it.

Distinction can be achieved by the use of unusual plant material, bits of color and line found in out of the way forms such as fern fronds, curling sprays of bittersweet berries or opening buds of maple in early spring. Look to nature for these suggestions. The fence row or open field will often produce real treasures. Don't be trite about what goes into your arrangement. Develop that "seeing eye" that finds beauty in unusual places. It will bring you more satisfaction than a charge account at the florists.

Distinction in flower arrangement is the creation of the outstanding through the unusual use of material, design and color. It is an indefinite something that raises an arrangement above the commonplace. It has good color, a nice choice of material thoughtfully combined in an appropriate container, plus a certain sense of fitness, and a sure knowledge of when to stop. Too few people use restraint. To have distinction be different, not eccentric, nor queer in your choice of vase or material or color combination, but be individual. You will not always find distinction but do try for it!

Besides the attributes already mentioned, now add *originality*. Make the arrangement truly yours by a personal touch that stamps it as your own.

CHAPTER 2

The Use of Color

THE theories of color harmony are more or less familiar to us all, through our daily use of color in clothing and decorations, and we have a fair idea of color harmony, even if we have not studied it in its theoretical aspects. But there are a number of considerations that must be borne in mind. Our color must dominate the arrangement. Care must be taken not to divide the interest too evenly between the different colors used. The more vivid the color used, the smaller its necessary amount. Hues of full intensity are much more dominating than shades, tones and tints. Lack of brilliance in color must be made up by the use of a greater amount of color. Dominant color is usually the focal point of the arrangement. It should be placed low near the rim of the container.

[11]

Colors should always be well grouped together, not spotted about or they will lose their value besides producing a freckled appearance.

Shades, tints and tones harmonize more readily than pure hues or colors, but the more dilute your color, the less vividness and zip your arrangement will have. Many people are afraid of color, and perhaps too many vivid color schemes would prove overstimulating, but an occasional orgy is good for anyone. Dark colors make lighter ones seem even lighter by contrast. In general, the darker the color is, the greater its apparent weight.

Of course the background, and the shape and size of your room must be considered. Simple backgrounds without too much design are most effective. The cool colors such as blue, green and light yellow have a receding effect while the warmer ones tend to stand out and bring your walls closer together. Warm colors are usually better in diffused and artificial light.

For a better understanding of the subject of color the use of a color wheel is advised.

There are two types of color which have very different properties. Spectrum colors are produced by breaking up the light ray into its component parts. They can be seen in the rainbow. The longest rays are the red, the shortest the violet. A combination of them all produces white light.

Pigment colors are produced by the use of pigments which absorb all of the light rays except those which cause the observed color of the object. These are reflected, and are perceived by our eyes which makes the object seem to have the color which we attribute to it. A combination of all the pigments theoretically produces black. It is with pigments that we are concerned.

Colors or hues are defined as primary and secondary. The primary colors are those which are "pure" . . . that is, they are not made by combining other colors. Red, yellow and blue are primary colors. The secondary colors are made by combining two of the primary colors. Orange, made with red and yellow; green, with yellow and blue, and purple with red and blue are considered secondary colors. The secondary color which contains the two colors lacking in the primary is called its complement. Complementary colors are opposite each other on a color wheel.

But we do not as a rule work with pure colors or hues for they are generally mixed with black, white or gray. Color which is mixed with black is known as a shade; a color which is mixed with white is called a tint; and a color which is mixed with gray, or grayed by the addition of its complement is a tone.

There are a number of color schemes that can be used in flower arrangements.

1. Monochromatic. Shades, tints and tones of one color, with green which can never be wholly eliminated from flower arrangements, and is usually disregarded. These arrangements offer danger in combining colors except in the case of red tones. Orange reds and purple reds do not usually blend well. Monochromatic arrangements are apt to be monotonous.

2. Analogous. Adjoining hues around the color wheel. Red, orange and yellow, yellow green and green are examples of analogous color harmony. These are a bit difficult but are apt to be more interesting.

3. Complementary. Opposite colors across the color wheel, colors which complete the spectrum. These are usually more satisfactory since the eye seems to need balanced color. Placing the color with its complement makes each seem brighter. There are several types of complementary color schemes.

a. Direct complements. Two colors opposite each other on a color wheel. If the primary colors are used the arrangement is more vivid and arresting. Direct complements are especially good for arrangements that dare to be seen at a distance.

b. Dual or split complements. Opposing hues, but not directly opposite. You choose the two shades on either side of the opposite one. As an example green is opposite red on the color wheel. If you were intending to use split complements with red, you would use blue green and yellow instead of plain green.

c. Triads. In this case use three colors which are complementary to each other. Red, blue, yellow are the simplest combinations, but many others can be figured from the color wheel.

d. Tetrads. Four colors equidistant around the color circle. These combinations are not effective except in mass arrangements where a large amount of material is to be used.

e. Contrasting. Colors of decided contrast, not actually complementary to each other.

Too subtle harmonies are not often good and must be carefully placed and well lighted to be effective.

In any color combination there should be a dominant tone with accents on one or more hues rather than an even division of color. The best effect is obtained by holding each color together in an interesting mass, rather than by dotting it about with other tones. This latter method will certainly lack distinction.

If adequate foliage is used most colors can be made to harmonize but often for the sake of design the use of foliage is limited. Gray greens will do much to make colors blend well if they are a bit difficult. Gray containers or backgrounds will accomplish the same effect.

Lighting has a very important effect on color in placing the arrangement in the home. The more direct and brilliant the light, the more intent the colors will appear, and the more dramatic the effect will be. Also if any lack of harmony is present it will be more pronounced if the light is especially good.

Proper distribution of color in your design can "make" your arrangement. Medium light and dark hues cannot be used "hit or miss" or the effect will be spotty and ineffective. They must be distributed carefully with real thought as to the design they will form.

Balance must be studied carefully in connection with color as well as form. An arrangement that is pleasing in its form design may be decidedly out of balance by improper distribution of color. Here we must remember the apparent "weight" of different colors. Almost always it is safest to use darkest colors low in the grouping — or toward the center if it is a horizontal arrangement.

Color plays a leading role in Harmony. It will often win a prize in a show even if the design is weak in the arrangement.

To achieve Unity it is not sufficient that the color scheme of the flowers alone shall be properly worked out. Containers, bases and backgrounds all contribute to the harmonious whole.

Rhythm must be carefully considered in working out a color design. The colors used should form a definite pattern and should produce a flowing feeling. If the color design can be made to follow the main lines of the design, it will add emphasis to the lines or rhythm of the composition.

Generally speaking, one hue should dominate the arrangement or set the key for the grouping. This can be supplemented by other hues either analogous or complementary, but these will play a definite subordinate part in the plan.

Too sharp contrasts are easily over-done. To be effective they must be well planned out.

In general the focus in the color design will be the same as the center of interest in the form design. If not there is apt to be a divided interest which will detract from the general effectiveness of the arrangement.

CHAPTER 3

Making the Arrangement

THERE are several important steps in putting your arrangement to-gether. You should first get a mental picture of what you are trying to do. A well thought out plan will be of considerable aid.

The next step is to select your material and container. An adequate mechanical control should be chosen which will hold your material firmly in place. Use plastacine or floral clay to fasten your holder to the container. Both clay and container must be dry in order to hold firmly.

Make yourself comfortable. Enjoy yourself!

The framework of your arrangement should now be assembled. Put in the foundation lines first. Start in with the high point and work out a silhouette. Now is the time to criticize and make changes, correcting any fault in balance and proportion. Next fill in all details. Be sure and get pleasing distribution of color. Use restraint. Stand back and make the final evaluation of your work. Look again for mistakes. Very often a close-up study will not show the faults, but from a distance faults in proportion, balance and placement are more evident. When the result is satisfactory, place your arrangement and leave it alone! Know when to stop!

What is left out is quite as important as what you put in your arrangement! Don't think you must use all the material you have cut. If you have nine roses and can make a lovely arrangement with five or seven, don't use the rest of them. Simplicity and restraint are always commendable. Don't crowd or bunch-up your material. Prune out any unwanted twigs and leaves that may spoil your line or plan.

Don't copy other people's arrangements, but adapt their ideas to your own use. If you see a good combination of material, or an interesting curve or line grouping use it to create your own arrangement. If you slavishly copy you get only a poor replica, for your material or container will probably not duplicate what you saw; but if you adapt it, you may make it a part of yourself and have really created something.

It is not what you have . . . it is what you do with it, that counts. Perfect material is not necessary. Often a deformed or irregular branch will make a more interesting arrangement. Make the most of what you have. Develop the "seeing eye" that finds beauty in common-place material. Be original. Combine what pleases you even though it is a bit unconventional. Don't be afraid of strong lines and bright colors. Be sure your material is well hardened before you begin. Use a variety of flower forms. They are more interesting if size and form are varied. Don't expect every arrangement you make to be a masterpiece. It won't be! Keep trying. Be honest. Analyze your grouping and see what is wrong. If you have the urge to go back again and again to change some element, you can be sure there is a mistake somewhere. Balance and proportion are apt to be your weak points.

Select a container of the correct size so that the finished arrangement will have a proper proportion to the space it is to occupy. Be sure the color will harmonize with the intended background. Then if there is color harmony in your flowers and container your whole arrangement will be effective in its surroundings.

An important consideration is the height of the place the finished arrangement is to occupy, whether it is high or low. In making a dinner table arrangement it is well to sit down while doing it — since the finished picture will be viewed by people who are seated. An arrangement for a hall table is usually viewed on three sides by people standing. Living-room arrangements must look well when viewed either seated or standing. If possible when doing a mantel grouping, work at it at the level it is to be when finished.

When you first began to make arrangements you no doubt felt inclined to copy or imitate those you had observed at shows or seen in books. This is good practice but does not make for spontaneity or originality. Your arrangements should have distinction and originality and *be individual!* No amount of practice and study will guarantee success in this particular, but careful training will do much to improve skill. We cannot all produce effects that are technically correct and truly original. This is a gift with which only the real artist is endowed by nature. Some of us excel in line, some in color, while others have a flare for texture and interesting combinations of materials. If you will make a conscientious effort you will go far and get much pleasure from your work.

First of all, you should have a plan or starting point for your arrangement. Get a mental picture of what you expect to do. Where will your mental picture start? Perhaps an unusual container will suggest an idea. Maybe the material will suggest the container. In any case what you want is an arrangement that is original and different, that will give your visitors pleasure in your home.

Use uncommon materials if you can. It is easier to get an "original" arrangement if the plant material or container, or both, are unusual. But do not be misled into thinking use of unconventional materials will assure an original arrangement. They merely make a hard job easier in that they are likely to suggest designs that possess originality.

Keep on the lookout for materials not too commonly used in arrangements — dramatic foliage, interesting seed pods, attractive rocks or weathered wood. All of these are aids to originality and distinction.

Your arrangement may well start with an accessory. Use care here however. The accessory may be novel and interesting, but unless it ties in with the arrangement in a subtle or dramatic manner it is not good. There must be unity.

Emphasis is another way to achieve originality. Do not try to use unusual plant material, a dramatic container and novel accessories all in one arrangement. You'll overdo the idea and probably fail to make a good arrangement besides. They can't all "steal the show." Let one part be emphatic and subordinate the other elements.

Finally check on these principles rigorously — design, scale, balance, harmony, focus, rhythm and unity. If your arrangement has all of these qualities it will be a good one.

CHAPTER 4

Types of Arrangements

WE have two general types of arrangements, mass and line. When we use large amounts of materials that are more or less solid, we have what is termed a mass arrangement. Even though we use a profusion of material, there is no excuse for crowding, although nearer the center of the grouping we naturally place the flowers closer together. Deeper color tones are best used here too. This aids in promoting balance. As we approach the edges we graduate sizes from half open blooms to buds.

Mass arrangements are distinguished by having a fine combination of colors and a definite center of interest. The effect is achieved by mass colors rather than by the excellence of any single flower. To be really effective they must be constructed according to a well thought out plan and not to be just masses of bloom stuck into a wide mouth vase.

An interesting silhouette will add much to a mass grouping. A broken outline is more attractive than a more regular one. Colors should be grouped to avoid a spotty effect. Mass arrangements are derived from the French, Persian, Victorian, Colonial and Modern schools.

Victorian Arrangements. These were heavy solid and rich, with many flowers of heavy, dark colors in upright, wide mouth vases which were often ornamented with raised figures and designs in gilt. They were filled with heavy masses of flowers, with accents in deep pinks, magentas and purples. They came from the Victorian age with its ornate schemes of decoration and the English climate with its many dull days, necessitating the use of the bright solid colors.

[17]

French Empire. These arrangements were also composed of masses of flowers, but they were usually arranged in lighter more airy containers which were often copied from Grecian vases. The flowers used were lighter in color, and were not so closely massed. Airy flowers, such as lily of the valley, narcissus, lilacs, roses and lilies are appropriate for this type of arrangement.

Colonial. These arrangements were also composed of masses of flowers, but simple, garden flowers were usually combined in containers of simple shape made from coarse pottery, copper, or pewter. Roses, verbenas, corn flower, bleeding heart, zinnias, pinks, marigolds and forget-me-nots are good for these arrangements.

In making mass arrangements, remember that in order to succeed you must have a definite idea in mind, a plan to work toward. You may find in the end that you have created something which is quite different from your original idea, but you still need an idea to begin with. In this type of arrangement, more than in any other, perhaps you must subordinate length of stem and beauty of individual bloom to the beauty of the composition as a whole.

Start your arrangement with the high point. Then block in your background, and locate your center of interest. Later add your supplementary masses. You may find it difficult to hold your color masses together, particularly if you are using flowers which have soft weak stems. This difficulty can be overcome by grouping several stems together and fastening with rubber bands before making final placement in the arrangement. *Remember,* you need restraint even in a mass arrangement.

Japanese Arrangements. The Japanese were the first people to practice the art of flower arrangement in a serious way. Through the long years since they began this study, they have developed a number of schools with more or less rigid rules, as well as an elaborate symbolism in the arrangement of flowers.

The beginner is apt to be frightened by the mere thought of attempting anything so intricate and rigidly controlled as a Japanese flower arrangement, and it would be foolish to try to copy arrangements which were developed by another civilization for houses which are so very different from ours.

It is true, however, that line and modern mass arrangements are developments which had their origin in the Japanese type of arranging, and in order to really understand them we must know something of it.

If you will look at a well made Japanese arrangement, you will find that each element of line, flower and leaf presented in it has a definite part to play in its composition, and none can be omitted without spoiling the effect of the whole. A few attempts at making simple

Japanese arrangements will teach the beginner a great deal about discarding superfluous material, and making each line "talk."

The Japanese have developed a great many different schools of arrangement, but all of them are more or less modified forms of the rigid and stylized classical type. They can teach us much.

Classical Japanese arrangements are built upon these lines:

1. *Primary line.* This is symbolic of Heaven. This is a naturally curved branch which must be once and a half the height of the container, or once and a half its dimension if it is shallow.

2. *Secondary line.* This is symbolic of man. It should be about half the height of the Heaven line and must come from the same base. This line may be composed of more than one stem. It may vary in height, but should always appear to come from the same base as the primary line.

3. *The Earth line.* This is about one-fourth of the height of the primary line, and must also appear to come from the same base. It is arranged inside the curve of the primary stalk.

The distinguishing features of Japanese classical design are: Asymmetrical balance, placement of three important levels, emergence of all stems from one stalk, the tip of the tallest bisecting its base, the employment of odd numbers, and the inevitable selecting of shrubs and flowerless trees.

The modified forms of Japanese arrangement are less severe than the classical type, in a number of important ways, although the triangular outline is always used. However, the use of flowering trees and shrubs, and other flowers is permitted, although it is usually restricted to three kinds in any given arrangement. The curves in the stems may be artificially induced by placing them under water for a short time and then bending them gradually between the fingers. The shortest or Earth line is permitted to emerge from a different point than the Heaven and Man lines.

There may be other elements and supplementary lines in the arrangement but they must never obscure the outline or the design which is always a tall, thin triangle. The groupings have little depth, but depend on outline and silhouette for their effectiveness.

The Japanese arrangement attempts to simulate growing plants of various heights with buds, leaves, and flowers in different stages of development. It is linear design embellished by leaves and flowers but never obscured by them.

Each leaf and flower must be an integral part of the design and contribute something to it, but must still be subordinate to the design itself. Crossing and interfering lines are removed, and flowers and leaves turned to display their most dramatic sides, until the picture is good to look upon but still retains the effect of a growing plant.

[19]

If you will study the pictures of Japanese arrangements, you will find that they often use plant materials quite different from that which westerners usually employ. The flowers and other plant material are almost always less showy than those which we would choose. They depend upon proper placing of line and perfection of arrangement for their appeal, rather than on massed effects or striking colors.

Line Arrangement. Line arrangement has a greater linear value than a mass grouping. It is much more difficult to do well, since the faults are more evident. In a mass grouping color is apt to hide many defects. In a line grouping we should use only what is absolutely necessary.

Line and silhouette are the important features of line groupings, but the formalism of Japanese arrangements is done away with. Allow the flower forms to suggest the shape of the arrangement. Select material with a definite line and use it to determine the character of your arrangement. Do not use too many lines or flowers. Restraint is imperative. Each element must be interesting and dramatic and of perfect form. In order to make a successful line arrangement, you must have an abundance of effective material to choose from. You should have a comfortable place in which to work, with good light and plenty of time. No nerves! A steady hand is essential.

Special Points in Making Line Arrangements.

1. Selection of branches, flowers, buds and leaves of interesting and distinctive form, texture and color.

2. Selection of container which harmonizes or contrasts with the plant material.

3. Careful placing of main lines.

4. Development of central point of interest.

5. Intelligent pruning of confusing and unnecessary twigs, leaves and flowers to give proper silhouette.

Line Arrangements May Be:

1. Vertical, with all stems pointing upward in ascending rhythm.

2. Horizontal, with stems extending horizontally from the mouth of the container.

3. Symmetrical, with both sides the same, as in an isosceles triangle.

4. Asymmetrical, with the two sides different but balanced.

5. Built on curved lines, semi-circles, circles and Hogarth curves.

Line flowers should have interesting, clear-cut dramatic shapes. Such flowers as calla lilies, tritomas, strellitzias, snowflakes, and gladioli are good. Branches of flowering shrubs and trees make excellent line material. Pussy willows, maple blossoms, hazel catkins, Scotch broom, as well as many grasses are good. Such leaves as those of the different irises, yucca, montbretia, acanthus and many others of strong and pleasing shape are valuable in line arrangements.

Modern arrangements. The term "modern" is perhaps a misnomer, since those styles which were termed modern a few years ago are already in discard, and are being followed by arrangements of an entirely different character. Perhaps the best interpretation of "modern contemporary" should be one which recognizes the right of each person to make arrangements of any type which suits his personality and looks well in the situation in which he intends to place it.

Most arrangements seen today are a combination of line and mass, and have been evolved by borrowing and adopting some of the features of both the Japanese and mass types of arrangements. This represents popular taste and seems to fit better in most present day settings. It employs beauty of line and silhouette and utilizes beautiful leaf and flower forms, but it also makes use of the best of mass arrangement principles giving weight and richness to the composition. It makes possible the use of more kinds of flowers than can be used in line arrangements alone, and gives more depth and solidity to the composition, yet the finished arrangement has the clear outlines taught by a close study of line work. Conservative modern designs may be said to blend line and mass in a happy combination which preserves the best of both.

As can be readily seen, this kind of arrangement offers great leeway in form and type. It provides for a background of line material of dramatic shape which may be balanced either symmetrically or asymmetrically, and which may be composed of almost any material which will give the desired texture, shape and color. This background may be constructed as carefully and with as keen an eye to form as any line arrangement.

To this as a center of interest, will be added a modified mass arrangement, which must be skillfully designed to embody the best features of the old type mass arrangement; that is proportion, focus, balance, and center of interest, as well as depth and good color combination. This must blend well with the background, and contrive to make with it, a unified composition which will express the personality of the arranger, and suit the surroundings in which it is to be placed.

Modernistic arrangements. These are made to conform with the most severe and formalized lines of the new type of architecture. They are often very striking, but are apt to have little depth, and may have very little beauty in themselves. They must have great strength of line, and a complete elimination of all unnecessary detail. As a usual thing, their beauty depends largely upon their basic design, with color as a secondary feature of less importance.

To obtain these qualities the plant materials used must have exceptionally striking shape. Combination of too many kinds of flowers are not good, as a confusion of forms detracts from the clear cut, bold line. Modernistic arrangements should be usually symmetrical in form.

using even numbers of flowers or sprays. Strong lines are essential. Do not use dainty feathery flowers. Have perfect balance always. These arrangements need not always be angular in form. The shape assumed will usually be decided by the container chosen. Round containers could well employ curved flower stems in a rounded effect, while square or triangular arrangements would employ vertical or horizontal lines.

Modernistic containers vary greatly in usefulness. Many are too conspicuous to be useful. Let them be beautiful in their simplicity of line, form and texture.

For this prim symmetrical handling, carnations, pom pom dahlias, irises, zinnias, calla lilies, stellitzias, red hot pokers, and such leaves as iris, yucca and acanthus as well as many kinds of succulents are excellent material. Such arrangements are apt to be stiff and a trifle unsympathetic . . . better for the flower show, where something striking and different is wanted than for the home, where more comfort is desired.

Remember that modern types of arrangements demand restraint. No unnecessary elements should be included in the design.

CHAPTER 5

Containers and Holders

IF you intend to practice the art of flower arrangement you must well consider the question of containers. You cannot expect to make interesting and beautiful arrangements unless you have containers which have good lines and pleasing shapes. This does not mean that you must spend a fortune for them, for they can often be had quite reasonably, but they must be carefully chosen and never purchased simply because they are a bargain.

Your lovely flowers need harmonious containers, but when you are selecting them pick out those which will blend well with the flowers and help to make a unified composition. A too conspicuous container immediately draws attention to itself, and away from the plant material in an arrangement, so that you have a bunch of flowers in a vase, instead of a picture in which all parts are subordinated to the whole.

When you are buying containers, be efficient and keep in mind the place where you intend to use them. You should not buy containers which will strike a jarring note. If you have Victorian furnishings in your home, you would naturally choose containers of a different type from those which would be used in a strictly modern house.

It is much better to have a few really good containers than many mediocre ones. If you are going to make arrangements it is imperative that you should spend money on one or two of your containers, at least. You do not need to buy a great many at once, but you can always have an eye out for the pleasing shapes, textures and colors. Be careful lest you unconsciously choose the same type or color of vase each time you buy one. If you are to be limited as to number, select only those that will have a general use about your home. Usually dull greens, warm browns or putty tones will have a wide usage. At any rate soft colors and dull glazes will be effective if the shape is good. A pillow vase, a shallow oblong rectangular container, and a rounded bowl or two of different sizes will always prove of value.

No directions can be given as to where only "good" containers can be found. Price is no criterion of beauty or usefulness. Our dime stores often carry excellent shapes and glazes. Second hand stores, good will shops and rummage sales may produce real "finds." Antique shops offer real possibilities. Look in the attic — you may find some treasures there.

If you have the space to store them, the gradual collection of containers will prove a delightful hobby. Soon you will realize what colors and glazes go best with your surroundings and you will cease acquiring white elephants. Buy when you see a container that appeals to you. It may not be in the shop when you come again.

Any container which is too conspicuous in color or form or texture is not desirable in making flower arrangements. Ornateness of shape or decoration will detract from the flowers and call undue attention to the container, thus spoiling the composition. A container should be something like a piano accompaniment to a violin or vocal solo; an element which is necessary to its completeness, but one which you feel unconsciously. Decorated pieces should be used as ornaments, or at best used to contain only simple leaf arrangements.

Receptacles of simple shape and plain soft colors are safest and easiest to use, especially for the beginner. If your budget for containers is strictly limited these are the kinds to choose, for tricky shapes and bright colors have at best a very limited scope of usefulness. Lately there has been quite a fad using objects which were made for other purposes as containers. Old oil lamps or churns are often to be seen holding flower arrangements. This is all right in moderation, but beware of using receptacles for flowers which were too obviously constructed for other uses.

Pottery containers of simple shape are usually the easiest to use. Those with a rough glaze are best suited for use with coarse or bold flowers, and should be used for the simpler, less studied arrangements. More delicate glazes demand finer quality flowers.

Metal containers are somewhat harder to use than pottery, but are often most beautiful when skillfully used. Bronze and brass containers are much easier to use after time has softened their harsh bright color to some extent. Bronze containers need bold fine colors and interesting forms. They are good for fruit branches and such large, definite flower forms as azalea and rhododendron blossoms. Pewter and silver are rather hard to use well. They demand fine flowers such as fine roses or orchids. Pewter-washed copper is delightful. Pewter is somewhat easier to use than silver, as it has a softer, duller finish. Three Zua irises with a cluster of forget-me-nots in a pewter bowl won a prize ribbon in a recent flower show here. Try an all white arrangement in polished silver. It can be stunning if well done.

Aluminum in simple shapes can be effective, though the finish is rather hard and bright. Even tin containers, when they have good lines and are not too shiny, are quite usable. Miners' gold pans make most interesting containers.

Glass containers really fall into two classes; those which are made from thick glass and those which are thin and delicate. The two types need quite different treatment, and demand very different plant material, but they have one difficulty in common, whatever type of flower-holder is used, it will inevitably show through the glass. Of course we are here discussing only transparent glass. Opaque glass is best treated like pottery. The stem pattern under water in clear glass is apt to prove difficult. Too many crossing stems are distracting.

Containers of heavy, thick glass, like battery jars and glass bricks, will take much heavier, bolder material than delicate, thin glass. Branches of fruit blooms or large, bold flower forms are best suited to these containers. Japanese glass floats or clear glass marbles are sometimes used in such containers to hold the flower stems in place or to hide the holder.

Thin, delicate glass will, of course, call for more delicate stems. Iceland poppies, fuchsias, clematis, and roses are all suitable for such use. Mexican glass is especially well suited for fuchsias. Flasks and plain glass cylinders are very good for many types of flowers. Colored glass is interesting, but beware of the vivid colors or off shades which will harmonize with very few kinds of flowers. Cut glass and crystal are not often flattering to cut flowers.

Simple, graceful shapes are much easier to use than those which are more ornate. The chalice shape is good, because it lifts the flowers up, and makes them seem important. Line arrangements usually need containers with simple severe lines. Low flat containers are the easiest to use when making such groupings.

Beware of vases which have too small openings. They will not hold enough flowers, and it is almost impossible to make a good arrangement when the plant stems are too crowded. Besides, the flowers will not be able to get enough water, and your arrangement will soon wither. If your water surface is large enough so that some of it is exposed to the air it will not foul so readily and the flowers will remain fresh longer.

Most baskets are very poor for arrangements. The handle is apt to be bad or the base is inadequate. At best they are useful for simple, artless arrangements, of such simple flowers as dahlias, goldenrod or asters, and at worst, they are bright colored atrocities tied with bows of baby blue or pink. If it is possible to find other types of containers, baskets are best left alone.

Holders. The important point in selecting a holder is to choose one that will be in harmony with our vase, heavy enough to hold the chosen flowers, but simple enough to be unnoticed in the finished arrangement.

Daisy holders and lead holders which are shaped like turtles or frogs are good, especially for use with large heavy stemmed flowers. If the flower stems are not quite large enough to stay where you want them you can wedge a small, extra piece of stem into the opening beside the flower stem to hold it firmly in place.

The needle point holder is one of the best for general usage. It is inconspicuous and, with practice, very efficient. If you have difficulty in making wiry or small stemmed material stay in place, try fastening a group of them together with a rubber band and inserting this group in the needles as one element. Often in making a focal point of small flowers this bunching idea is a good one, since it holds them together more easily and firmly. Fasten your holder securely to your container with plasticine. If both container and holder are dry you will have no difficulty in securing stability.

When deep glass containers are used a different type of holder is necessary. Narrow strips of sheet lead can be bent to fit around the stems and hooked over the rim of the container. This device can be hidden by an overhanging bit of foliage or cluster of flowers. For a wide-mouth glass container, crumpled chicken wire can be fastened over the mouth of the container and the flowers arranged through it. For cylindrical glass you can make a good holder by pleating a narrow strip of hardware cloth or rat wire so that it will fit in the mouth of the container. Beware of molded glass or pottery holders equipped with straight up and down holes. They make a very stiff arrangement with a picket-fence effect.

For the deep pottery container perhaps the simplest procedure is the use of bushing. Before you fill your vase with water, take a handful of brake fern or other rough greenery such as long hedge clippings or bits of shrubs and pack it into the vase with the stems in a vertical position. The greenery can then be cut off level with the mouth of the container. The proper amount of bushing to use soon comes with experience. If you use too much you will have difficulty inserting the stems of your arrangement material, while if you use too little you will be unable to make the flowers stay where you want them. Whatever sort of holder you use, be sure that it is invisible in the finished arrangement. Weathered rocks can be used with needle holders in shallow containers, or leaves or blossoms can be arranged so as to hide them. In a taller glass container, the arranging of a trailing spray or bloom down over the edge of the container will hide the holder and do much to tie the arrangement together, thus providing better unity. In clear glass, sprays or clusters of foliage can be placed low to hide the mechanical control before the arrangement itself is made.

For better stability in large arrangements — especially when made at home and transported to a show — heat the holder slightly and if the bottom of the container is also slightly warm the floral clay will hold much more firmly and there will be more assurance of it staying put. This is a good idea when large or heavy flowering material is used in any flat container about the home. It is most aggravating to have a grouping almost completed and then have it topple over.

CHAPTER 6

Figures and Accessories

FIGURES and accessories must be used with great care and restraint. When you have used a figure as a part of an arrangement, it is a good idea to remove the figure and stand back and look at your arrangement. If it looks as well without the figure — leave it out. Never stick a random figure into an arrangement, hoping that it will improve the design. It won't! Unless your figure is an integral and necessary part of the design, you will be better off without it.

If you are fond of collecting figures, keep them in a cabinet. There is no place in an ordinary arrangement for such figures as Ferdinand the Bull or Figaro regardless of how cute they are in themselves, and as for unclad china nymphs dancing before ornate mirrors and such, please leave them out.

The safest way to use a figure is to create a background for it from your container and plant material, always bearing in mind the situation in which the object represented by such a figure might be found.

With your figure as a starting point you can choose a container and plant material which will harmonize with it in color, texture and feeling as well as size. One very important thing to remember is the size of your figure in relation to your plant material, or you may be reminded of Edward Lear's limerick —

There was an old man who said "Hush,
I perceive a young bird in a bush,"
When they asked, "Is it small?"
He replied, "Not at all,
It is four times as big as the bush."

Don't be ridiculous unless you are purposely trying to be funny. Remember that scale is very important in the use of figures.

Your figures should be of a type which will blend readily with your background and help to make a good picture. Avoid accessories which are too brightly colored and have too high a lustre. White figures are apt to be conspicuous and must be used with great care. If you are buying a Madonna be sure that the expression is sweet, serene and calm. Some of our more modern Madonnas express too much sophistication. Chinese figures of the more sober type are usually good.

Do not allow your figurines to stand in the water unless they are types which would naturally be found there. Ducks, fishes, and even fawns and fishermen could well be placed in the water, but other types of figurines need a base of rocks or other material to stand on.

If you do use figures, use a flat plate or a low container of simple lines with little ornament, but with a fine color and use only a few blooms and be particular about your scale so that the relation of the flowers to the figure and the container is pleasing.

Sometimes an arrangement needs a figure outside the container to help balance it properly. Here again, great care should be exercised, and a figure used only if it is really necessary to the completion of the design. Do not develop the habit of spotting figures and accessories about. Many a good arrangement has failed to take a prize because the arranger added too many accessories. Almost always they are better omitted. Do not place them where they can be easily overturned.

Rocks can be used in a number of ways and often add much to the appearance of an arrangement. They are regularly employed in shallow containers to hide the holders, but we are here discussing their use as an integral part of the main flower picture. They may be very effective when used this way and give balance, solidity, and a fine naturalistic feeling. It goes without saying that they are to be used in informal arrangements only. They are of particular value in winter, when arrangement material is scarce.

The rocks used must be chosen with great care. Dark colored rocks are usually best, since they give weight to the composition and must necessarily be the heaviest thing in it. Either red, gray or black rocks are good. Weathered, pitted or mossy rocks blend most satisfactorily with plant material to produce atmosphere and interest. Never use polished agates.

Wood may be used in two ways. Large, weathered pieces may be used much the same way as large rocks to give stability and weight to your arrangement. Gray twisted driftwood branches, polished satin smooth by sand and sea water are especially effective when used in pottery or pewter plates. They provide much interesting line material. Smaller weathered branches, either bare or draped with moss or lichens, are often very good to provide interesting background and silhouette in an arrangement of flowers. They are especially handy to use in winter when plant material is apt to be scarce. It should be understood that arrangements with rocks and wood should be used only occasionally, since they may become tiresome if used too often.

Wooden blocks or rounded discs as bases for arrangements are useful in promoting balance, down low, where it is most necessary. Blocks of wood in various thicknesses may be used and they may be painted to contrast or harmonize with the container, or stained and waxed to show the grain of the wood. Kalsomine or cold water paint can be applied to both base and container if a particular color scheme is desired. It can be washed off when no longer needed. Footed teakwood stands when obtainable from the Orient, are delightful for use, but simple homemade bases can be very effective. Plywood circles in varied sizes and colors are attractive when used beneath or behind a flower grouping. Bamboo rafts in light to dark brown tones are effective for bases or backgrounds, and natural palm fiber mats will help to make an attractive frame for many arrangements.

CHAPTER 7

The Use of Unusual Material

THERE is always an element of danger in using new and untried material in flower arrangements, but there is also a sense of adventure which lends zest to the use of unusual plant forms. It is so easy to get into a rut and use the same sort of material over and over again, that it is a good idea to attempt to branch out by using less common material.

There are three general ways in which unusual effects may be achieved. First of all the use of unusual material — plants, weeds, leaves and seeds which are not ordinarily considered suitable for flower arrangements. Second, it is possible to use more familiar material in unusual ways, and third, uncommon combinations offer a welcome change from more stereotyped arrangements.

It must be understood, however, that the mere use of uncommon material does not suspend the principles of flower arrangement. Good taste must be observed no matter what sort of an arrangement we are making. Don't use material simply because it is "different," without considering the room in which it is to be used and the position it will occupy. A well executed arrangement of extraordinary material is most striking, and it can be a distinct addition to the room in which it is placed, but unless it is most carefully constructed, the result may be anything but pleasing. If you decide to use "different" material, you must realize that you will have to proceed very carefully, or instead of making lovely arrangements that are different, you will only succeed in making fantastic messes that are distressing.

But if you will persevere in your attempts, you will be rewarded in ways you have not even considered. If you will learn to look about you with the "seeing eye" you will be surprised at the wealth and variety of material lying close at hand. Even if you never achieve any great degree of success in your arrangements, you will have gained immeasurably in your ability to see beauty of color, line and form where you least expect to find it.

It is a lot of fun to experiment with new material, too, and the best of it is that you can find most of it growing by the roadsides; so you won't be out any money, even if our arrangement turns out to be hopelessly queer. Every roadside and vacant lot is a treasure house of material. The humble Queen Anne's Lace, the lowly horsetail, plumy grass blossoms, sour dock seeds, rushes, alder catkins, the possibilities are wellnigh inexhaustible. If you turn to the garden, there, too, you will find much material which you have overlooked when you had only the conventional type of arrangement planned.

Let us consider, then first of all, the use of wild waste material, which we find in every field and fence row. The possibilities of Queen Anne's lace are sufficiently evident to even the most hide-bound conventionalist, but some day try combining it with green and white ribbon grass, in a round full-bodied vase of dull green or blue, and see what a cool, refreshing picture it will make.

A light, airy, pyramidal arrangement of these same flowers without any foliage in a white china compote makes an arresting centerpiece. Graduate the sizes of the flower heads using the heavy ones low in the grouping. By using different stem lengths, depth and shadows can be produced and contribute greatly to the pleasing effect of the arrangement.

Try making a modern line arrangement by simply using three sprays of mature horsetail in assorted lengths in a rectangular white container about an inch high. A few weathered rocks and a life-like frog figurine will add interest to the group. The same sort of container can be arranged with two groups of sedges which are in blossom. Place the taller group at the back of the container to the right, and a smaller shorter group at the left front. If well done, it will have distinction and a certain style all its own. When you are gathering wild material, it is a good idea to pick some long grass plumes. You will find that they sometimes come in handy to soften the lines of your composition, or give height to your arrangement. But use them with restraint for they may confuse your lines or blur the outlines of your design.

When we come to the unusual arrangement of garden material we are more handicapped by conventional ideas, but even here, there is some latitude if we will learn to free ourselves of preconceived notions. The grand sweepstakes prize in a recent spring show was an arrangement of Siberian iris leaves with green hellebore blooms and the pale silvery green seed heads of the white anemone pulsatilla. They were arranged on a rather deep plate of creamy yellow with the iris leaves in a fan at the back. In front of them were seven fluffy seed heads of the anemone in uneven stem lengths. The focal point was a handsome cluster of the lovely chartreuse green hellebore blooms with some small weathered rocks covering the frog and giving more width at the base. It was very simple and restrained, and yet strikingly effective.

Green hellebore blossoms are very useful in many types of unusual arrangements. They are attractive in bud, blossom, or seed and last a long time for use. Try arranging them with sprays of Cornus Mas on a green Celedon plate. They are also very effective when used with such bulbous plants as snowflakes and the green and white flowers of Ornithagalum Nutans.

There are certain types of flowers which make better arrangement material, when all or part of their leaves are removed. You will find that lilacs are much more lasting when their leaves have been cut off, for they wilt long before the flowers do. Mock orange is always better for a little judicious pruning, as this allows the waxy white flowers to be seen in all their beauty. The fruits of the wild Indian peach are really lovely when they have been freed of their leaves, so that their warm tones of orange red and purple can be properly appreciated. Do not hesitate to take off leaves or surplus blossoms, if you think that the beauty of your arrangement will be enhanced thereby. Only be sure that it will! Don't try to be too painfully different.

Unusual combinations of material offer perhaps the widest scope for unusual arrangements. Do not be daunted by the fact that you have never seen certain materials used together. If colors and textures are harmonious and will combine to make a unified, coherent whole, put them together and take pleasure in the result, even if it is different from anything you ever saw. Do not be afraid to combine fruit and vegetables with your flowers. A focal point of grapes and apples at the rim of the container can be very effective in an arrangement of autumn flowers. Oriental kale with its curled and crested foliage and its creamy lavender or pink tones can be striking in a low rectangular container of dull bluish green. Place the kale off center toward one corner of the container on a low needle holder and combine with sprays of lavender winter flowering heather. This arrangement will last for several weeks.

Autumn furnishes much unusual combination material. Here is one variation seen at a recent flower show. In a large spherical Chinese vase of golden yellow tone, tall fluffy pampas grass plumes formed a fan in the background, while sprays of rattlesnake grass and dried seed pods of lunaria with pale yellow mums, made up the foreground. At the edge of the container were grouped two yellow apples and a long bunch of yellowish green grapes. It was a fine study in monotones and was called "Gentlemen Prefer Blondes."

Foliage bouquets, too, come under the head of unusual combinations. A glass battery jar makes a very attractive container for mass arrangements of foliage. Copper and brass are particularly fine for broad-leaved evergreens and berries. Autumn colored leaves are always lovely, of course, but a little study of the forms and textures will help you in making this kind of composition. Stiff pointed leaves, like those of irises, hosta (day lilies), or arums are very good for background and accent. Avoid using leaves of too similar shape and textures, or your arrangement will lack distinction.

Very interesting line arrangements are also possible with foliage alone, curved sprays of Japanese maple, copper beech, and many other trees and shrubs offer inviting possibilities. You can do wonders along this line with succulents; they have such distinct and unusual forms. Try using some of the spiky ones for background in a flat container with the rosetted, rounded forms in front.

Develop your "seeing eye." You can find many possibilities all about you if you will but look for them.

CHAPTER 8

Photographs

IN the illustrated section are presented, by seasonal groupings, many examples of flower arrangement made by the author. Simple, inexpensive garden flowers and plants have been used to show an interesting combination of materials, which we hope will be an inspiration to the reader.

With each photograph will be found a short description of the arrangement with comments on container and material.

SPRING

SPRING finds the flower arranger impatient for early bloom after the long winter. Flowering shrubs, bulbs and early perennials all invite a wider range of their wealth of color, form and texture. Truly the enthusiast finds in this abundant season a period of delight.

Line arrangement. White bowl with Goddess of Mercy and pale pink double prunus blooms. Note how the curved sprays follow the line of the figure. White stone chips cover frog and base of figurine for better unity.

(Upper Left)

Andromeda japonica and Golden Spur daffodils in a soft yellow bowl. The teakwood base adds width and weight. Andromeda with its attractive foliage, buds and blooms is delightful at any season of the year.

(Upper Right)

Ascending Rhythm using long upreaching lines and a tall cylindrical container. Pale yellow Sir Watkin daffodils with rose red camellias in a clear pale blue glass chimney beaker. Note how the lowest camellia comes down over the edge of the glass for better unity.

(Opposite Page)

Hogarth curve. Cornus mas and forsythia make up the upper part of the curve, King Alfred daffodils in yellow and chartreuse Helleborus Corsicus form the center of interest. Arum italicum foliage gives weight and width. A Persian brass melon vase is ideal to set off the yellow green combination of materials.

(Upper Left)

Bronzy leaved Saxafraga Megasea inspired this arrangement. An ascending rhythm of Yucca leaves complements the sprays of early yellow jasmine and the first Golden Spur daffodils. Flat pewter container. Balance is made more interesting by placing a larger grouping of Saxafrage leaves at one side of the central axis and balancing it by the heavier mass of daffodils on the opposite side.

(Upper Right)

Yellow Hogarth curve in brown pillow vase. Forsythia, bronzy tinted retinospera foliage and Sir Watkin daffodils in a sandy brown pillow.

(Opposite Page)

Modified mass grouping. Snowflakes, white hyacinths and white narcissus in an iridescent blue green glass bowl. The difference in shape and texture of the flowers adds interest in the composition.

(Upper Left)

Snowflakes, white daffodils, blue Roman hyacinths and pulmonaria, Mrs. Moon in a white bowl. Cool blue and white effect warmed up by the pinkish buds of the pulmonaria. Placing the bowl off center on the black wooden base adds variety.

(Upper Right)

Cinnamon brown Italian vase. Snowflakes and white camellias. Freshness and simplicity is the keynote of this arrangement.

Here seaweed fans and camellias combine to produce interest. A warm soft blue bowl goes well with the camellias. There is a hint of blue in the fully opened flowers, and the lavender blue tones of the mid rib of the fans ties the whole composition together. Note textural interest and repetition of rounded forms.

Weathered wood, bleached and polished by wind and sun,
has many interesting possibilities for arrangement material.
Use your "seeing eye" when at the beach or mountains for
good pieces. Silvery rhododendron roots found in a burnt
over area are used with shell pink camellias in a white
rectangular bowl. Their exotic shape and lovely texture
make a fine foil for the waxy blooms.

Little rock garden composition. A naturalistic grouping of early materials. Soft blue Queen of Heaven primroses, deep rose colored hardy cyclamen Atkinsii blooms and foliage, with red to bronze toned geranium japonicum and weathered gray rocks. Form and color of the chosen leaves are as important as the blooms.

Black and white arrangement for mid spring. Dainty Scilla italica with double spirea blooms and buds. At the base of the grouping shiny black pieces of coal add distinction and contrast to texture. Note how the sprays of buds lighten the effect low near the rim of the container.

(Opposite Page)

Easter season. All white, using three types of bloom with a madonna in a square china compote. Snowflakes, Roman hyacinths and white daffodils. The stems of the snowflakes repeat the curved line of the bowed head of the figure to suggest the arch of a church window.

All white arrangements may have distinction and charm. Here we have used the waxy white double spirea blooms as a background for the white figurine. The sweep of the folds of her garments are repeated in the movement of the flower placements, some of which are placed in front to make foreground as well as background for the figure. Be sure to keep the flowers in scale with your figurine.

A pale blue chop plate forms the base of our arrangement. The aged figure dressed in dull and pale yellow is seated on gray weathered rocks. Andromeda japonica sprays in buds to full bloom make up the background for the figure. Their drooping panicles repeat the lines of his clothing.

An all white grouping with stone chips covering needle holder. Branches
are in varied planes to give depth.

(*Opposite Page*)

Lilacs and Poets narcissus in an antique white bowl. Triangular form in
a free standing arrangement without foliage.

(Upper Left)

A soft yellow plate, gray weathered rocks, a piece of dogwood root with pink berried pernettia sprays and a seated figure make up our composition. Soft tones of pink, gray, brown and green form a delicate and pleasing color grouping.

(Upper Right)

Pussywillows with early yellow jasmine give us a real spring feeling. A matching yellow bowl and a yellow, blue and green bird continue our color. Weathered rocks at the base of the grouping give weight and balance.

SUMMER

SUMMER brings us an entirely different grouping of materials than we had earlier in the season. Colors are more intense and bloom is more abundant.

A study in radiating lines using white and green materials to produce early summer coolness. White Siberian iris for height and width with creamy white peonies for focal point give pleasing variety in form. Variegated funkia leaves with silvery grass heads add line interest and weight.

A dull blue gray cylindrical vase holds this brilliant grouping. Yellow Spuria iris buds form the tip of the triangle, at one side lower down are yellow Spanish broom and the ruffled Spanish iris, Golden Lion. Allium Moly in showy clusters is backed up by saxafrage leaves and frames the focal point of wide open iris blooms. Note depth and shadows.

(Opposite Page)

Roadside flowers. Soft pink spires of wild spirea combined with marguerites in a deep blue green pillow vase. The spirea blooms are arranged in graceful radiating lines forming a triangular background for the focal point of daisiies. Note graduation in stem lengths to give depth and shadows to the grouping.

(Upper Left)

Curly thistle foliage with feverfew and Regal lily blooms combine with iris foliage and the old seed heads of sisyrinchium to carry the rounded forms high in the grouping. The container is a crackle glaze chartreuse bowl which repeats the color of the taller material.

(Upper Right)

Cool gray and white grouping. A pyramidal freestanding arrangement using various textures. The airy ribbon grass combines well with the heavy white perennial peas and the lacy chiffon daisies. The gray foliage of the santolina adds width and coolness. The old white china compote with its graceful sturdy lines is well suited to such a grouping.

(Lower Left)

A blue bubble glass chimney beaker holds hemerocallis Calypso with the foliage of funkia sieboldii. The funkia leaves have good form and texture, and are heavy enough for the rather large day lily blooms. To hold the material in place we used crumpled wire at the top of the vase. This forms an inconspicuous holder which can be hidden by a leaf or flower.

(Lower Right)

Siberian iris leaves and blooms with saxafrage leaves and allium blossoms in a leaf shaped container. Medium blue iris with lavender alliums and the plum to rosy lavender lining of the bowl make a pleasing effect. Variation in form and texture add interest and silhouette.

Onions and roses and brake fiddle heads. Extremes meet here in a delightful grouping. The container is a soft chartreuse with a brown over glaze. The color is carried up into the arrangement by the immature fern fronds. The onion blooms are a soft amethyst color, while the roses, the old-fashioned Perle d'Or, are yellowish apricot. These flower forms are essentially the same in outline and size but their textural and color interest make them good material to combine. This is a free standing grouping.

(*Opposite Page*)
This yellow yarrow arrangement captures the spirit of growing plant life. The rhythm of decreasing sizes of the clusters as they progress upward is satisfying. The relation of various flower heads is irregular but orderly in the build up of the design. Little foliage is used. The deep yellow plate exactly matches the material.

A natural colored split bamboo tray is used for a grouping of flowers and vegetables. White radishes, green peppers, an artichoke, and several small squashes are combined with snowballs, double spirea and allium neapolitanum. A needle holder placed in a shallow container which holds water is hidden by the material and keeps the blooms fresh.

(Lower Left)

Deep blue Siberian iris with roadside grasses and grape hyacinth seed heads form a simple but satisfying grouping. Ruffled primrose leaves are effective at the base.

(Lower Right)

Don't say you have no arrangement material. The roadside will provide if you have but the "seeing eye." Choose variety of forms—feathery grasses, airy lychnis, wild daisies and foamy plumes of meadow sweet with the foliage of wild rue. A cool, light and airy arrangement is the result. Use the lightest material high and the larger and more open flowers low at the center.

(Upper Left)
Cool colors for a hot day. A dull soft blue bowl with sprays of butterfly bush and rosy magenta perennial peas in a pleasing movement of curves. Note how the highest spray sets the scheme for the whole grouping and with the lowest placement of peas makes a reverse curve.

(Upper Right)
Japanese iris used with sprays of green dock seed in an upward movement. A spiral placing of the iris blooms in a triangular silhouette. The lavender container with its soft blue lining combines nicely with the iris of the same lavender tone.

Free standing arrangement of pale pink peonies with silvery thalictrum glaucum foliage in a spiral movement. The container is heavy textured with a soft blue green color and is very useful for large or heavy blooms.

An empty prune juice bottle in clear green glass makes a delightful container in spite of its humble origin. Its weight, shape and texture are all well suited to the arrangement of coral pink gerberas with their own foliage. The irregularly swirled leaves have good form and texture and their undulating curves add much to the design. Angle and variety in under water stem lengths will add pattern to any clear glass grouping. Be careful of crossing lines here that may blur your design.

Dianthus Inchmary with thalictrum glaucum in a pink lined blue rectangular bowl. Inchmary is a melting pink colored sweet scented dianthus which should be more widely grown. The silvery thalictrum foliage is delighful with it.

Silvery grass plumes, pale pink to lavender toned allium blooms and white sprays of Fabiana imbricata in a blue bowl show radiating movement. Roadside grasses with their delicate form and color can do much to give a light and airy quality to an arrangement. They can add height without weight and will do much to improve silhouette if used with care.

(Upper Left)
This triangular design is worked out in warm shades of yellow, green and brown. The yellow bowl exactly matches the rudbeckia blooms. The flower stems stand briskly erect above the massed heads at the base. A rising feeling is repeated in the foliage curves. The horizontal plane of most of the flowers adds to the movement of the lines.

(Upper Right)
Hen and chickens, euphorbia and montbretia leaves in a deep pewter plate. A triangular design in gray, greens and pink. A focal point of hen and chickens rosettes with their soft pink to gray green blossoms grouped above and flanked by the silvery foliage of euphorbia myrsinites makes a rich and subtle blending of delicate colors.

An amethyst Mexican glass plate with its radiating pattern is used as an in-between meals decoration for the dining table. In it, at one side, are grouped three creamy yellow Mermaid roses and foliage. In making plate arrangements do not cover too much of the surface or a crowded effect is produced.

Late summer glory. Rudbeckia, golden glow and golden
rod in a heavy pottery bowl of warm brown. For more
weight and width the arrangement is placed on a brown
bamboo mat. Note how each element is grouped together
— the fluffy golden rod is used high, the heavier golden
glow is placed low in front, while the rudbeckias on the
right with their dark centers add interest and movement.
A few sprays of hardy geranium low on the left bring the
material down over the edge of the bowl and tie the whole
ensemble together.

(Upper Left)

A combination of curves and angles. Funkia Thomas Hogg is our arrangement material. The bowl has a plain blue lining and the outside color is slightly deeper in tone than the soft lavender funkia blooms.

(Upper Right)

A heavy Chinese pottery bowl in blue black on a bamboo raft holds a combination of Siberian iris Periwinkle and lavender onion blooms. The onion blooms are small so are grouped closely to equal the color mass of the iris blooms.

FALL

HARVEST time brings the arranger a wide variety in color and form. Fruits and vegetables can be the inspiration for many attractive combinations with foliage and flowering material.

An interesting study in round forms. Wine to deep purple pompom dahlias with camellia foliage and round green and white striped gourds arranged in a low pewter bowl. Note the graduation in sizes as the flowers are placed high in the grouping. Repetition of form is brought out in the round bamboo logs in the raft.

Twin mantel grouping. Simplicity is the keynote especially for the summer season when a feeling of coolness is in order. A pair of sand colored pillow vases hold our brown to yellow materials. The highest elements are sprays of bronze to copper dock seeds. These form a nice color contrast to the deep yellow of the heliopsis and the softer toned hemorcallis which make up the focal point. For weight, width and rhythmic movement we have used gerbera foliage on either side of the arrangements. These leaves are placed slightly higher on one side than the other to forward the upward swing of the material. Much will depend on the background of your mantel as to what will look well on it. Flowers near framed pictures are apt to prove distracting if they divide or confuse the interest. Mirrors are easy to handle as they reflect the flower arrangement.

(Upper Left)

Bishop of Llandoff dahlias in a low white bowl are used as a background for the white Chinese devil dog. The brilliant velvety red dahlias with their black stems are most dramatic when used with all white accessories.

(Upper Right)

Late summer color. A heavy dull blue bowl of simple lines and good texture admirably sets off the gay colored materials in it. Buff to orange pompom dahlias with light yellow to deep orange zinnias in varied sizes are grouped to make an attractive ensemble. A cluster of small green to yellow quinces at one side gives a feeling of autumn.

A pale yellow plate with Baby Royal dahlias in salmon
pink, red toned snowball foliage and clematis seed heads
make up a charming bit of late summer color. The focal
point is made up of a group of velvety textured quinces in
yellow green tones which with the silvery seed heads and
delicate colored blooms form a rich and colorful grouping.
A similar cluster of quinces on the back side with three
dahlias above them make this a freestanding arrangement.

Salmon colored Picardy glads are used with green to orange-red seed heads of arum italicum as a focal point. Heavy gray green gerbera leaves give weight and good texture. The heavy rectangular bowl has a fine gray green color and will find many uses throughout the season.

Lemon yellow pompom dahlias in a matching bowl. Note how little foliage is used to give a pure color effect. The triangular form is maintained by placing this freestanding arrangement diagonally across the bowl and finishing up both sides of the grouping in a similar manner.

(Opposite Page)

Deep orange to copper bronze dahlias in a cinnamon brown bowl are here used with a few sprays of orange montbretia. Careful selection of buds and half open flowers add interest. Andromeda foliage ties the arrangement to the container. A few recessed blooms add light and shade by their proper placement.

Baby Royal dahlias, saxafrage and monbretia leaves and seed heads of arum italicum in a blue green elongated container. Shrimp, salmon and yellow tones in the dahlias are pleasing with the green orange and yellow of the seed spikes.

(Upper Left)

Pale pink snapdragons, deeper pink Margery Emberson dahlias with begonia leaves in a pale yellow vase.

(Upper Right)

Slender pale yellow glads with their own foliage form the high point of our grouping in a close vertical placement. The foliage in varied lengths emphasizes this upward movement. Massed hydrangea blooms are grouped at the rim of the container. These in their prime were blue, but now late in the season are a delightful soft green. Three gray green gerbera leaves break up the mass of the hydrangeas.

[75]

(Upper Left)
Brown Siberian iris seed heads, autumn shaded snowball foliage with
Spanish broom and cactus dahlias in a gray green bowl. A triangular
pattern of rich autumn shades.

(Upper Right)
Margery Emberson miniature dahlias with heather blooms and white
broom foliage in a soft raspberry colored bowl. We selected white broom
foliage for its lovely gray green color instead of the common broom
which has a yellow green tone. The heather is a soft orchid color while
the dahlias are a vivid rose with a hint of salmon in the center. Note
the radiating movement in the broom and heather sprays.

(Opposite Page)
Vertical movement. Dark brown earthenware Chinese wine jar with
yellow to red high brush cranberries and giant montbretia foliage and
orange blooms.

A natural colored split bamboo tray is here used as a centerpiece with deep yellow crooked neck squashes and green grapes, yellow to orange nasturtiums. and deep orange montbretia blossoms. Silvery sprays of euphorbia myrsinites add textural value. The flowering material is kept fresh by placing a needle holder in a flat container which holds water and is hidden by the blossoms and fruit.

Gay English golden rod with autumn tinted azalea foliage and round headed yellow dahlias make up a colorful grouping. Grapes and apples give a fall atmosphere and blend nicely with the dull blue container. They extend the line of the arrangement toward the base of the cylindrical vase on its mahogany stand.

An oval chartreuse container with lemon pompom dahlias, buff to soft pink coxcomb, greenish brown montbretia seeds and a warm brown piece of wood for the high point. Bronzy corylopsis foliage adds a nice textural note.

(Upper Left)

Brownish green montbretia foliage with deep brown iris pods combined with red bronze azalea foliage make a colorful background for a grouping of autumn tinted cactus dahlias. Chinese arbor vitae with its silvery brown cones varies form and texture.

(Upper Right)

Hogarth curve in a powder blue bowl. Gray green dried palm foliage with curly kale and the silvery blue heads of globe thistle. Our focal point is a large pale lavender dahlia and bud which should have photographed a darker tone. Note how the shorter palm leaf with the lower kale leaves makes a pleasing reverse curve.

A blue green rectangular bowl holds a corner grouping of liatris, perennial aster and dahlias. Varied lengths of the rosy magenta liatris furnish the outline for the grouping. Fluffy sprays of the tiny sulphur yellow aster luteus give variety in size and form and add to the radiating movement. Small yellow to orange tinted pompoms and three large ball dahlias give further size interest. These latter are pale yellow with bronze edges and form the focal point of the arrangement.

(*Opposite Page*)
An all green arrangement will prove cool and refreshing. A bright yellow vase with a background of rosemary sprays and yucca leaves with Queen Anne's lace seed heads. The focal point uses very green apples and green grapes with begonia leaves to add width. Don't be too conventional, try something different.

Green Siberian iris pods with their foliage form our tallest placement. Andromeda leaves give weight and heavy texture. White to green heads of hydrangea Hills of Snow are placed low in the grouping. In their prime these were a waxy white but with age they turn a lovely soft yellow green color.

Outline or silhouette is of utmost importance in flower
arrangement. Try not to use the same form over and over.
The crescent offers a pleasing variation. Here we used early
bronze chrysanthemums in a low pewter vase. To soften
the outlines we have added sprays of clematis foliage.
Buds and smaller flowers are used at the tips, while wide
open blooms give central weight.

(Upper Left)

A mass grouping of irregular outline in a brown pillow vase produces fall color and interest. Salmon glads, yellow, buff and deep orange mums in several forms, combine with a cascade of fall fruits over the edge of the vase.

(Upper Right)

Pale to deep pink snapdragons grouped with silvery pink mums in a flaring raspberry tone bowl. For more weight we place the bowl on a black glass stand. Heavy flowers are grouped low for better balance.

(Opposite Page)

Interesting containers may be found in unexpected places. A pale yellow coffee server holds curved sprays of bittersweet with autumn colored single mums.

Dramatic foliage gives a striking effect with fruit and flowers. A fan of yucca leaves makes up our high point, while an aralia leaf gives further form interest and weight. Spidery pale yellow mums tie the fruit and foliage together. The center of interest is made up of two green artichokes. These are flanked by green pears, yellow green grapes, green peppers and green tomatoes in varied sizes.

Single yellow mums in a simple grouping with Japanese maple foliage in autumn tints in a dull blue cylindrical vase.

Winter twigs make up this radiating movement. Various
evergreens with hazel catkins are grouped about our focal
point of pine cones.

WINTER

COLDER weather limits our flowering material but develops the ingenuity of the arranger. Fruits and berries find good uses at this season

---

Horizontal grouping in a low crackleware pillow. Sprays of witchhazel with their golden brown blooms form the horizontal placements, while pine foliage and a group of brown cones make up the focal point.

Fruit and flower centerpiece. A bamboo mat with blue and tokay grapes, red apples, rusty brown pears and red-bronze mums makes up a colorful grouping for a low decoration. Flowers and foliage can be arranged to hide the flat container which holds the water and frog. Eggplant, artichokes, bananas, and various citrus fruits and nuts will all combine nicely with flowers or even with foliage alone to produce an attractive grouping. A diagonal placing of the arrangement on a tray or mat may prove of interest. Study color and form for dramatic combinations.

An old putty colored stein with a pewter lid is used for this winter grouping. Silvery juniper with its blue berries and pink pompom mums give good line and movement.

(Upper Left)
This completed arrangement was actually only 7 inches tall. A soft brown
pillow with andromeda foliage placed low, and mountain ash, various
ornamental crabs, holly and bayberries to give form and color in yellows,
orange and red combined with the gray of the bayberries. The tall gray
green foliage is that of a small species rhododendron.

(Upper Right)
Winter berries can add cheer to your home. Here we have placed berries
and leaves of skimmia in a low pewter vase. Curved Scotch broom foliage
adds line interest. The combination of the shiny red berries with the
deep green foliage and the pewter bowl is good.

Witchhazel branches with pine sprays add line interest to a grouping of orange colored citrus fruits in varied sizes. Bronzy boxwood tips tie the orange fruits and the brown witchhazel together. A natural colored bamboo mat supports the grouping.

Dried arrangement. A dull pewter bowl with a grouping of "wooden" roses, Empress tree seed heads and magnolia leaves in a triangular motif. The focal point is made up of roses while the seed pod clusters give a rising feeling. The warm brown tones of the different materials combine nicely with the container and the dark brown bamboo mat.

(Lower Left)

Another dry grouping using much the same material as in the preceding arrangement but with a different feeling. Yucca leaves and bare bitter-sweet twigs give height and movement. A dark brown earthenware Chinese wine jar holds our arrangement.

(Lower Right)

A few grouped sedges arranged in three levels, together with a few weathered rocks and bits of moss make a good background for our three white ducklings. The deep pottery plate exactly matches the bright orange color of our ducks' beaks.

An all foliage grouping. Slender gray green yucca leaves with white veined arum italicum foliage frame a rosette of gray velvety mullein in a pleasing textural grouping. The bowl is a soft blue gray color with deeper blue over glaze.

The vegetable garden can often furnish good arrangement material. These cabbage rosettes are side shoots that developed after the main head of cabbage had been cut earlier in the season. Their flower like form and delicate "bloom" make them good accents for the placement of dull green yucca leaves and pink heather sprays. The lavender and pinkish tones in some of the cabbage leaves pick up the opalescent tints of the bowl.

Winter crescent. If arrangement materials are very scarce one can always rely on evergreen sprays and cones to bring a bit of color indoors. Their soft subdued tones can be delightful in the proper setting. A low pewter pillow is here used to make up a simple crescent shaped grouping. Silvery toned trailing juniper sprays serve to form the outline while the focal point is made up of a group of brown cones.

Brown toned group. A deep brown pottery plate is the foundation of
our grouping. Chocolate brown magnolia leaves give weight low and
follow the line of the satiny brown dogwood stick on the left side of the
arrangement. As a focal point we placed three yarrow heads at different
heights to emphasize the upward lift of the composition. For variety and
form the empty brown seed heads of grape hyacinths are effective while
some dry tumble weed is grouped at the left front.

Bayberries with bronze to green foliaged cotoneaster humifusa are here used with a pale blue fawn in a matching blue bowl. A few small red cotoneaster berries near the frog add weight and color but keep in scale with the figure.

Late winter bloom. A deep pewter washed copper plate is here used with gray weathered wood combined with pink heather and deep wine colored heleborus purpureus. Heathers are delightful material for arrangements and may be had in many forms for either winter or summer bloom.

Trailing juniper with Christmas rose blooms and cyclamen leaves. In a gray blue toned flat container are grouped the lovely heleborus niger or Christmas rose blooms with the ivy shaped marbled foliage of the hardy cyclamen. These form the focal point of the crescent which is made up of the blue gray trailing juniper. Both heleborus and cyclamen in their several forms are cherished for their winter bloom, when little else will brave the elements and produce their welcome color.

Blue juniper and gray bayberries are grouped with weathered rocks, on a heavy pink plate. The droll Kay Finche owl is somewhat iridescent and will pick up surrounding colors so that on the pink plate it has a definitely pink tone.

(Upper Left)

Blue fawn in a blue bowl accented by a cluster of pink heather and deep wine colored helebore blooms.

(Upper Right)

If you can't find any flowers — try fruits. A deep yellow toned pottery plate is here centered with leafless Japanese quince twigs with their yellow to pink freckled fruits. Rhododendron foliage has been added at the base of the group for width and weight. When brought indoors in winter these quinces have a delightful fruity aroma and will prove a charming addition to the living or dining room.

Soft creamy pink mums in a dull rose colored bowl. Curved sprays of pine give us a more pleasing silhouette. The use of many buds and half open flowers gives variety in size which adds interest.

(*Upper Left*)

Christmas breakfast. On a round Rye Krisp from your grocery store group holly sprays with grapes, apples, lemons, limes and nuts to form a simple but different centerpiece.

(*Upper Right*)

Fruits and berries in an ivory colored shell with a pinkish colored lining. Long slender aluminum curls have been used with the fruits for distinction and sophistication. They prolong the curves and help to lighten the rather heavy material. The fluted shape of the shell is repeated in the placement of the bananas. Here curved sprays of pink snowberry add line and color and develop a Hogarth line with the fruit and curls on the wooden disc under the shell.

A pale green candle with gray green yucca leaves gives dramatic outline to this grouping. Cotoneaster franchetti sprays with their red-orange berries add graceful curves and a touch of bright color. Bronzy toned saxafrage leaves give richness and weight while the focal point of Christmas rose blooms make it a charming holiday decoration. Our bowl is an oblong gray green pottery container which is especially suited to this arrangement.

(*Upper Left*)

A study in round forms. Three plywood circles painted in three values of dull green are here used with a fat pale green candle and a grouping of green grass bubbles at the base of our Madonna. A background of juniper sprays with round pearly berries carries the rounded form up into the arrangement.

(*Upper Right*)

Somewhere in your home at Christmas time have a little shrine that will depict the glory of the season. This arrangement was planned for a mantel grouping with a burning candle in the center. It is garlanded about with delicate evergreens, bits of heather bloom, pink pernettia and pepper berries. A cluster of three very tiny hemlock cones adds weight and focus at the front. The kneeling figures are made of crackleware with a pleasing finish. Their mood is quiet and reverent and lends a serene and lovely touch to the group.

A tall pale green candle with a pink berried evergreen garland is placed in a low pink octagonal bowl. Heather blooms and pink pepper berries wreath the base of the candle.

Pine branches and cones. Curved branches were selected to give a wind-blown movement using materials typical of the season. A bright tomato-red chop plate is used as a container and the combination of orange-red, green and warm brown is most pleasing. Brilliant color in arrangement material is not imperative. Often delightful effects can be produced with a vivid container and more somber material. Good lighting is imporant if dull colors are used.